A quick look at the Sun

What is the Sun?
The Sun is a star. It is a ball of very hot gases that gives off heat and light.

Where is the Sun in our solar system?
The Sun is in the centre of the **solar system**. Everything in the solar system circles the Sun.

How far is the Sun from the Earth?
The Sun is an average of 149 million kilometres (93 million miles) away from the Earth.

What colour is the Sun?
The Sun is a yellowish white star.

How big is the Sun?
The Sun is about 1,400,000 kilometres (870,000 miles) in **diameter**.

What are sunspots?
Dark spots and bright spots dot the surface of the Sun. Dark sunspots are cooler parts of the surface. Brighter spots, called plages, are hotter parts of the surface.

What is a solar eclipse?
The Moon passes between the Earth and the Sun during a solar eclipse. The Moon blocks sunlight and throws a dark shadow on the Earth.

Our Sun is only one of billions of stars in the sky. The group in this photo contains millions of stars.

The Sun in the solar system

The sky is full of stars. A star is a giant ball of very hot gases. Most stars look like little specks of light from the Earth. Only one star looks big and bright. This star is called the Sun.

The Sun is only a medium-sized star, but it looks larger and brighter than other stars because it is the closest star to the Earth. The Sun is about 149 million kilometres (93 million miles) away from the Earth. The next nearest star is roughly 270,000 times further out in space. The Sun would seem small and dim if it were further away from the Earth.

Living things on the Earth would die without the Sun. The Sun gives off light and heat. People, plants and animals need this light and heat to live.

Centre of the solar system

The Sun is the centre of the **solar system**. The solar system is the Sun and all the objects that circle it. Our solar system is made up of nine planets and 101 moons. Smaller objects also circle the Sun. Comets are balls of rock and ice that have long tails of glowing gases when they near the Sun. Large rocks called asteroids also circle the Sun.

The Sun is the largest object in the solar system. It is about 1,400,000 kilometres (870,000 miles) in **diameter**. The Earth is much smaller. It is only 12,756 kilometres (7926 miles) in diameter. More than 1 million Earths could fit inside the Sun.

The Sun's gravity holds the solar system together. Gravity is a natural force that attracts objects to each other. All the objects in the solar system pull on each other because of their gravity. Massive objects, such as stars and planets, have greater gravity.

Gravity makes objects circle the Sun in paths called orbits. Each of the nine planets orbits the Sun at a different distance. The planet Mercury has the closest orbit to the Sun. Pluto usually has the furthest orbit from the Sun.

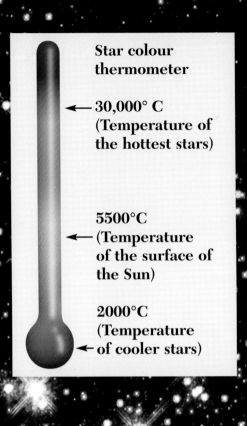

Star colour
thermometer

← 30,000° C
(Temperature of
the hottest stars)

5500°C
← (Temperature
of the surface of
the Sun)

2000°C
(Temperature
← of cooler stars)

Stars are different colours, depending on
how hot they are.

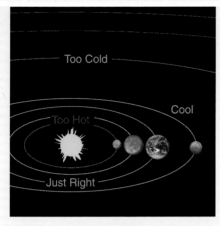

The perfect distance

Venus is closer to the Sun than the Earth. It receives twice as much sunlight. Thick clouds surrounding Venus hold the Sun's heat. At its surface, Venus is about 480°C (900°F). That is twice as hot as an oven can get. The Earth is at the perfect distance from the Sun for living things. Its average temperature is 17°C (62°F). Mars is too cold because it is further from the Sun than the Earth. Its average temperature is –57°C (–70°F).

Star colours

Stars can be different colours. A star's colour tells **astronomers** how hot it is. Astronomers are scientists who study objects in outer space.

The hottest stars are blue. Their temperature is about 30,000°C (54,000°F). Cooler stars are red. The temperature of red stars is about 3000°C (5400°F).

Medium-warm stars are yellow. The Sun is a yellow star. Its surface temperature is about 5500°C (9900°F). This is 21 times hotter than an oven. The Sun is just the right temperature and distance from the Earth, so living things can grow.

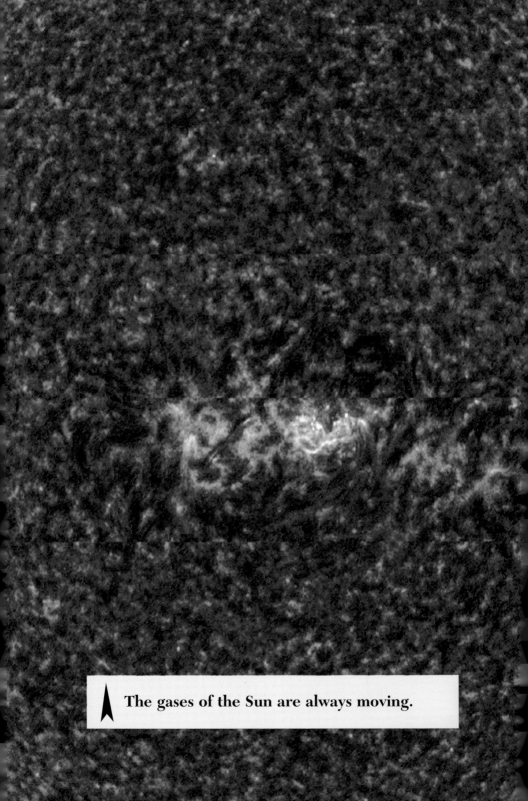

The gases of the Sun are always moving.

Parts of the Sun

The Sun is made of layers of very hot gases. A person would not be able to stand on the Sun. It has no solid surface.

The centre of the Sun is called the core. It is about 400,000 kilometres (248,560 miles) in **diameter**. Gravity and the weight of the outer layers press the gases inside the core. This makes the gases thick, heavy and hot.

The Sun's core reaches a temperature of about 15 million°C (27 million°F). This great heat would immediately turn a person into dust. The Sun's light and heat are made in the core. The light and heat travel from the core to the outer layers of the Sun.

The radiative zone is a thick envelope of cooler gas that surrounds the core. Energy zigzags through this zone like a ball in a table tennis game.

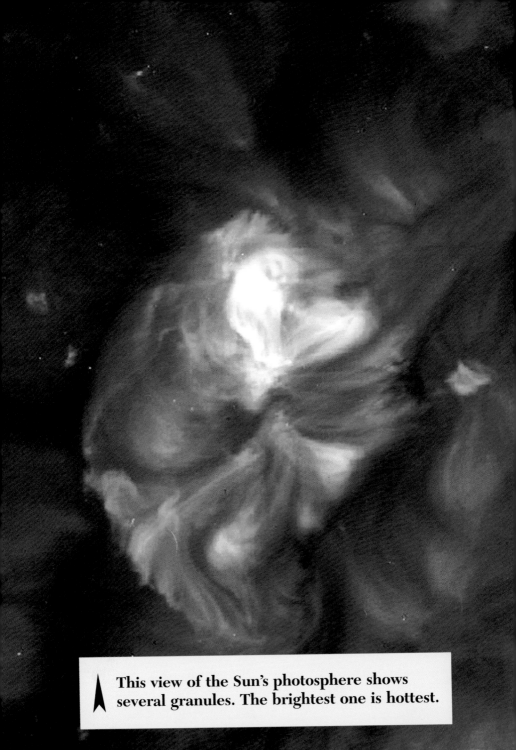

This view of the Sun's photosphere shows several granules. The brightest one is hottest.

Convective zone

The convective zone is the second layer of gases that surrounds the Sun's core. It has large cells of moving gases. The cells rise upwards to the surface.

Heat and light from the Sun's core travel upwards through these cells. Because the Sun is so large, this journey through the radiative and convective zones to the surface can take millions of years.

The photosphere

The **photosphere** is the surface of the Sun. This layer of hot gases is about 300 kilometres (200 miles) thick. The photosphere is the part of the Sun people see from the Earth. It releases most of the Sun's light and heat into space.

The photosphere is an active place. Hot gases are always bubbling to the surface. This makes the photosphere look like a pot of boiling soup. Hot gas bubbles, called granules, form at the tops of cells from the convective zone. Most granules are 1000 to 2000 kilometres (600 to 1200 miles) in **diameter**.

Most granules cool at the surface. Then they sink down and become part of the lower photosphere. New hot gas bubbles rise to the surface and make new granules.

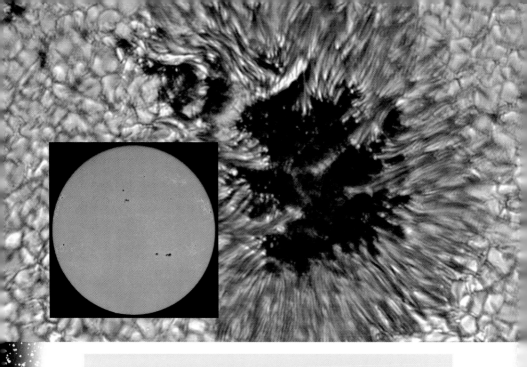

This photo shows a close-up view of a sunspot. The dark areas on the Sun (inset) are sunspots.

Sunspots and plages

Sunspots are cooler areas of the **photosphere**. Sunspots are about 1000°C (1800°F) cooler than the rest of the surface. Their cooler temperature makes them look like small, dark circles. Each sunspot usually lasts several days.

Small sunspots are between 1000 and 2000 kilometres (621 and 1243 miles) across. Big sunspots can be many thousands of kilometres across. The big spots usually have dark centres and lighter edges.

The number of sunspots on the Sun changes over time. The change in the number of sunspots is called the sunspot cycle. The number of sunspots goes up and down during this cycle. Each sunspot cycle lasts approximately eleven years.

Plages are hotter areas of the photosphere. They look like bright spots on the Sun. Plages are a lot like sunspots, but they are hotter areas of the surface. They usually last several days.

Studying sunspots

Astronomers never look directly at the Sun with just their eyes. The Sun is too bright and would harm the human eye. Instead, Sun telescopes project pictures of the Sun onto screens. Astronomers can see sunspots as dark areas in these pictures.

Astronomers can use sunspots to measure the Sun's spin. They pick a big sunspot and watch it every day. The Sun's spinning makes the spot seem to move across the Sun from left to right. The spot eventually disappears behind the Sun. Later, it reappears on the left edge of the Sun. Astronomers know the Sun has spun once when the spot returns to its original place.

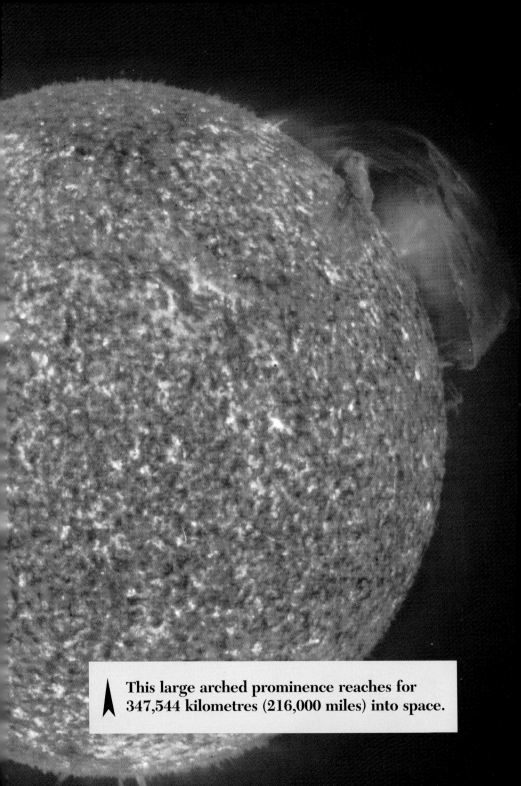

This large arched prominence reaches for 347,544 kilometres (216,000 miles) into space.

Prominences

A magnetic field surrounds the Sun. A magnetic field is an area surrounding an object that has the power to attract metals and other electrically charged particles. The magnetic field comes from moving liquid gas inside the Sun. The movement generates electricity that travels in currents inside the Sun. Electric currents create the magnetic field.

Scientists use magnetic field lines to show how magnetic energy flows. Some of the Sun's magnetic lines loop around its surface. Other lines shoot into space.

Scientists believe the Sun's magnetic field causes explosions. Sometimes the gas is blocked from flowing past the field lines. Energy from the gas builds until the gas explodes into space. These huge columns of flaming gas are called prominences.

Prominences shoot into space. The gases can travel hundreds of kilometres per second and can extend hundreds of thousands of kilometres above the Sun's **chromosphere**. In time, they fall back to the **photosphere**.

Prominences can have two different forms. Sometimes they look like fiery fountains of gas. Other times, they look like large arches. The middle of the arch hangs in the Sun's **atmosphere**.

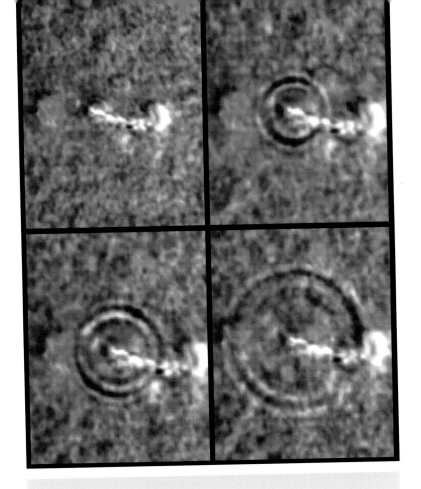

This series of photos shows the spread of a sunquake. The white flash is a solar flare. It causes a sunquake. The sunquake's waves grow larger as they ripple over the surface.

Solar flares and sunquakes

Solar flares are large explosions on the Sun. They often occur over sunspots or areas with a lot of magnetic energy. The magnetic energy builds until a flare explodes. Large amounts of burning gases blast from the surface. The gases speed through space.

Solar flares are much larger and more violent than prominences. The explosions are often larger than the Earth. They rip the **photosphere** apart. A flare is like millions of bombs going off all at once. Flares can last for a few hours.

Solar flares can cause sunquakes. Waves of energy move out from solar flares in circular patterns. **Astronomers** can see these waves on the surface of the Sun. They view the sunquakes from the Earth through special telescopes.

Sometimes sunquakes cause deep rumblings that shake the Sun. The shaking echoes underneath the Sun's surface. It continues until the entire Sun vibrates.

Explosions on the Sun can affect things on the Earth. Sometimes gas particles from solar flares reach the Earth's **atmosphere**. This can cause static on radios, TVs and cordless telephones.

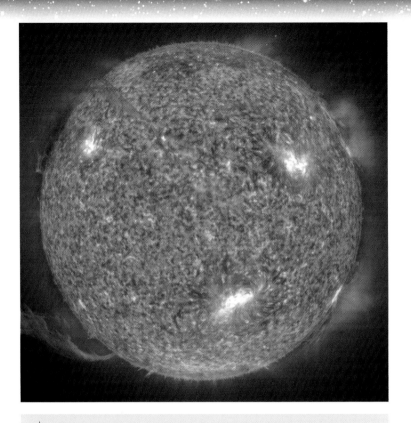

Flaming gas bursts through the chromosphere.

The Sun's atmosphere

Above the **photosphere** is the **chromosphere**. This is the Sun's inner **atmosphere**. The chromosphere is about 4,000 kilometres (2500 miles) thick. The chromosphere appears pink near the Sun's surface.

Gases in the chromosphere are always moving. The moving gases form spikes of gas called spicules. These fiery jets of gas shoot into space.

▲ **This picture shows the thin gases of the corona spreading into space.**

The Sun's outer atmosphere is called the **corona**. It is a wide layer of gases surrounding the Sun. The corona is much hotter than the Sun's surface. Temperatures can reach up to 3.5 million°C (6.3 million°F). The corona can stretch out millions of kilometres from the Sun.

The corona changes shape. Sometimes it is round. At other times, it has points and large bumps. It is hard to see the corona because the Sun's light brightens the sky.

The gases in the corona are very thin. Some of them leak out into space. These streams of escaped gas particles are called the solar wind. A solar wind moves outwards from the Sun at speeds of hundreds of kilometres per hour.

Green plants use sunlight to make the food they need to grow. Animals, such as this frog, need the Sun's warmth to survive.

Light and heat

All stars send light and heat into space. Bigger stars release greater amounts of light and heat. How far the light and heat travel into space depends on how big the star is. The Sun's light travels throughout the **solar system** and beyond.

Only a tiny fraction of all the Sun's light falls on the Earth, but it is enough to make the Earth a good place to live. Sunlight warms the air, ground and oceans of the Earth. It makes plants grow. Sunlight drives the winds and makes rain fall.

Sunlight spreads out and weakens as it travels further from the Sun. Sunlight is very dim by the time it reaches Pluto. Daytime on Pluto is as dark as night-time is on the Earth. The Sun does not warm Pluto so it is always frozen.

How the Sun makes light and heat

The Sun is made of different elements. Elements are pure materials found in nature. About 75 per cent of the Sun is the element **hydrogen** gas. About 25 per cent is **helium** gas. Other gases make up only a tiny part of the Sun. The Sun uses its gases as fuel to make energy.

The Sun makes its energy by turning hydrogen atoms into helium atoms. An atom is the smallest part of an element. The process of turning hydrogen into helium is called nuclear **fusion**. Fusion takes place in the Sun's core.

Nuclear fusion joins two elements into one element. Hydrogen is made of small pieces called protons. The great heat and pressure in the Sun's core squeeze the hydrogen protons together. Sometimes the protons stick to each other. When this happens, the protons build a new atom of helium.

Energy is left over after fusion happens. Some of the extra energy is released in the form of light and heat. Every second, the Sun turns millions of tonnes of hydrogen into helium and extra energy. The energy from this process slowly travels to the Sun's surface. Then it shoots out into space as light and heat.

 It takes millions of years for energy to reach the Sun's surface. Then it shoots into space.

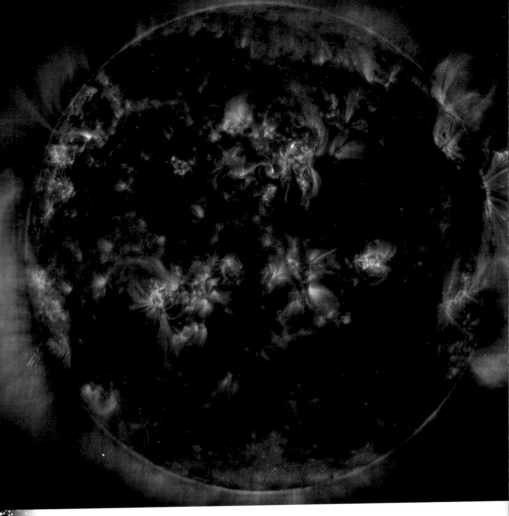

Invisible light

The Sun radiates, or sends out, different kinds of energy. Energy from the Sun moves through space in waves or rays. People can see only some waves given off by the Sun. They can see light rays called sunlight, but there are some kinds of rays that people cannot see.

Explosions on the Sun's surface can send X-rays and ultraviolet (UV) rays into space. UV rays and X-rays are invisible waves of light energy from the Sun. X-rays are so powerful that they can pass through objects that common rays of light cannot pass through.

X-rays and UV rays from the Sun are harmful to people. They can burn people's skin. The Earth's **atmosphere** acts like a shield. It protects us from most of the Sun's X-rays and UV rays.

Astronomers study X-rays given off by the Sun. To see X-rays, astronomers use satellites. A satellite is a machine sent into space to orbit the Earth. Satellites collect information and send it back to the Earth. Some satellites collect X-rays or UV rays to take pictures of the Sun.

Astronomers study these special pictures of the Sun. The pictures show different things than normal pictures. For example, X-ray pictures show large plages on the Sun. UV pictures show active places in the **chromosphere**.

Sun time

1 Earth orbit = 1 Year

1 Earth spin = 1 Day

A day equals one Earth spin and a year is the time it takes the Earth to orbit the Sun.

The Sun and the Earth

Every day, the Sun seems to rise in the east. It appears to move across the sky during the day. At night, the Sun seems to set in the west. But the Sun is not really moving around the Earth. Instead, the Earth rotates, or spins. The spinning Earth makes the Sun appear to move across the sky.

Astronomers in ancient times used the Sun's position in the sky to measure time. They measured the time from sunrise to sunrise to find out how long one day was. A day is the time it takes for the Earth to spin around once.

The Sun was also used to measure a year. The Earth's orbit around the Sun makes the Sun appear to move through the stars in the sky. Astronomers measured how long it took the Sun to reach the place in the sky where it started. Astronomers discovered that it took about 365 days. This means that it takes the Earth 365 days to orbit the Sun.

> **Winter is caused by the Earth tilting away from the Sun.**

Summer and winter

Much of the Earth's weather is cold for part of the year. Sometimes snow falls. The air is also warm for part of the year. Plants grow during this time. These different periods of weather are called seasons.

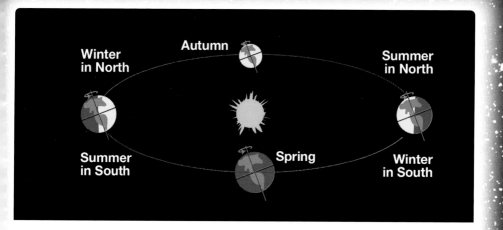

Winter in North
Autumn
Summer in North
Summer in South
Spring
Winter in South

This diagram shows how the Earth's tilt causes seasons as it orbits the Sun.

The Earth has seasons because it tilts as it orbits the Sun. During summer in the Northern Hemisphere, the northern half of the Earth is tilted towards the Sun. Longer days and direct sunlight warm the northern half of the Earth, making it summer there. In the Southern Hemisphere, or southern half of the Earth, days are shorter and sunlight is indirect, making it winter there.

During winter in the Northern Hemisphere, the northern part of the Earth is tilted away from the Sun. Then it is winter in the northern half of the Earth and summer in the southern half.

Blue skies and sunsets

The sunlight people can see is made of seven colours of light. The colours are red, orange, yellow, green, blue, violet-blue (called indigo) and violet. The colours of light mix together to make white light.

People use prisms to see the different colours of light. A prism is a special piece of glass that is shaped like a triangle. White light that passes through a prism separates into the seven different colours of light.

Colours in sunlight scatter when they enter the Earth's **atmosphere**. Some colours zigzag more than others. Blue light zigzags the most. The blue light seems to come from all directions in the sky. This makes the sky appear blue.

The Sun appears low in the sky at sunrise and sunset. Sunlight must travel through more of the Earth's atmosphere to reach the Earth. The atmosphere blocks the blue, indigo and violet light. Most of the green and yellow light is blocked, too. The remaining colours that make it through to the Earth turn the sky orange, pink, gold and red at sunset.

This sunset is orange and gold because other colours of light have scattered in the thick air.

Auroras

Sometimes material from the Sun lights up the night sky. Faint blue, red or green lights may appear. These lights are called auroras. The lights look like colourful bands or blowing curtains.

The solar wind causes auroras on the Earth. Solar wind contains electrically charged particles from the Sun. Like the Sun, the Earth has a magnetic field. Some of the Sun's particles get caught in the Earth's magnetic field. The magnetic field guides particles from the Sun towards the Earth's North and South Poles. When the particles strike the Earth's **atmosphere**, they glow. This glow is like the light from a neon sign.

The particles move around the atmosphere, causing more glowing. This makes the aurora seem to dance.

People have nicknames for auroras. When auroras appear near the North Pole, they are called Northern Lights. When auroras appear near the South Pole, they are called Southern Lights.

 This picture of the Southern Lights was taken from a spacecraft orbiting the Earth.

Viewing eclipses

Never look directly at the Sun, even during an eclipse. Its light can hurt your eyes, even if you wear sunglasses. Scientists must use special solar filters to look at the Sun during eclipses.

Solar eclipses

A solar eclipse happens when the Moon passes between the Earth and the Sun. During a solar eclipse, the Sun's light is blocked.

As the Moon moves between the Earth and the Sun, its narrow shadow falls across the Earth. People must be right under the shadow to see the eclipse. In a few minutes, the Moon passes directly in front of the Sun. Within the Moon's shadow, the day seems to turn into night because the sunlight is blocked.

Sometimes only part of the Moon blocks the Sun. Then the Sun looks like someone has taken a bite out of it. This is called a partial eclipse. At other times, the Moon completely blocks the Sun. This is called a total eclipse.

Total eclipses can be exciting. All of the bright glare of the Sun is blocked. Scientists can use solar filters to get a rare look at the Sun's pink **corona** for just a few minutes.

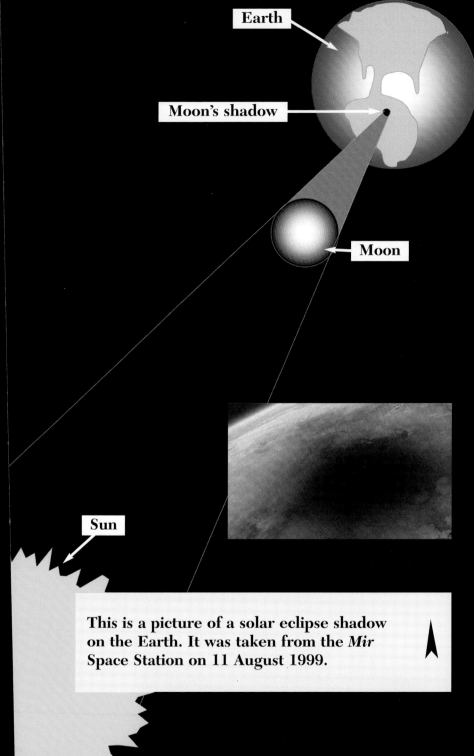

Earth

Moon's shadow

Moon

Sun

This is a picture of a solar eclipse shadow on the Earth. It was taken from the *Mir* Space Station on 11 August 1999.

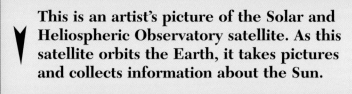

This is an artist's picture of the Solar and Heliospheric Observatory satellite. As this satellite orbits the Earth, it takes pictures and collects information about the Sun.

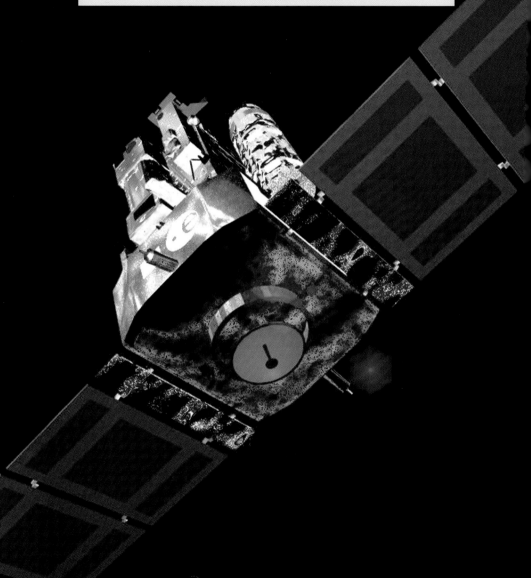

Life cycle of the Sun

Astronomers want to learn about the life cycle of the Sun. They want to know how the Sun formed and when it will die. Astronomers use many tools to study the Sun.

Solar telescopes are important tools. They are large tubes. A mirror at the top of the telescope aims sunlight down the tube. The sunlight travels hundreds of metres and reflects on a screen. The Sun appears as a large circle on the screen and sunspots show up as dark areas on the circle.

Other solar telescopes study the Sun's **atmosphere**. These telescopes have dark discs. The discs are moved exactly in front of the Sun. By covering the Sun's bright **photosphere**, astronomers can study the **corona**.

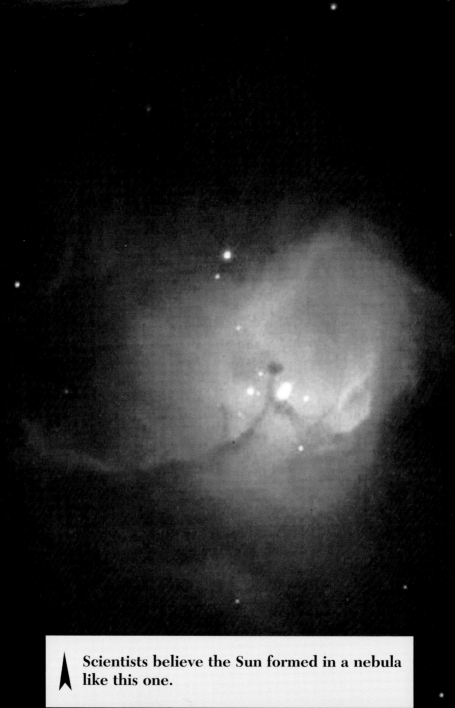

Scientists believe the Sun formed in a nebula like this one.

Some satellites carry solar telescopes. It is easier to see the Sun from space than from the Earth. There are no clouds in space to block the view. The satellites send information from the solar telescopes back to scientists on the Earth.

How the Sun formed

Most scientists believe the Sun formed about five billion years ago. They think it began in a cloud of gas and dust. Clouds like this in space are called **nebulas**. Scientists think the nebula that the Sun came from was trillions of kilometres wide.

After time, the gas and dust in the nebula began to fall into its centre. A nearby star exploded. The force of the explosion pressed the nebula's gas and dust closely together. The gas and dust began to stick together into a clump. The clump grew as more and more gas and dust stuck to it.

The gravity of the clump of gas and dust created great pressure on the middle of the clump. The inside began to heat up. The gravity attracted more gas and dust and a giant ball formed.

After a long time, **fusion** began in the centre of the clump. The Sun was born. Fusion made the Sun glow and solar wind blew the remaining gas and dust away.

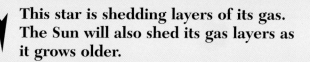
This star is shedding layers of its gas.
The Sun will also shed its gas layers as
it grows older.

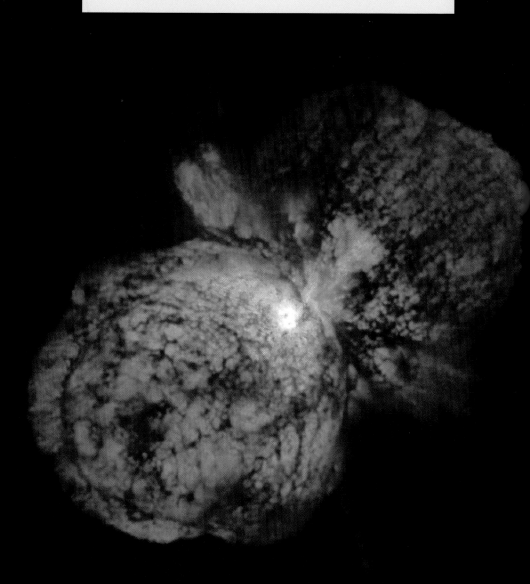

The future of the Sun

Stars live for billions of years and then die. Our Sun will die like other stars, but it will take a long time for this to happen.

Scientists believe the Sun will cool down after time and then it will begin expanding. It will probably become between 50 and 100 times larger than it is today. Then it will be a red giant star.

As the Sun grows, it may swallow up the planets Mercury and Venus. If this happens, life on Earth will no longer be possible. The Earth's surface temperature will increase to approximately 1200°C (2200°F). The water in the oceans will boil away.

The Sun will eventually run out of **hydrogen** gas to turn into energy. Then the Sun's outer layers will blow into space and form a **nebula**. The Sun's remaining core will shrink. The Sun will become a tiny white dwarf star about the size of the Earth and it will continue to cool. The remaining planets in our **solar system** will freeze.

People on the Earth will enjoy the Sun for a long time to come. The Sun is a middle-aged star. It is only about five billion years old. The Sun will not die for several billion years.

Glossary

astronomer scientist who studies objects in space

atmosphere layer of gases that surrounds an object in space

chromosphere (KROHM-uh-sfear) inner layer of the Sun's atmosphere

corona outer layer of the Sun's atmosphere

diameter distance from one side of a sphere or circle to the other, passing through the centre

fusion process where two elements fuse together into one, creating energy

helium second lightest element found in nature; helium is a gas often used to make balloons float

hydrogen lightest element in nature; hydrogen is an odourless gas

nebula (NEB-yoo-lah) huge cloud of gas and dust in space

photosphere (FOE-toe-sfear) surface of the Sun

solar system all the objects that orbit around a star

Websites

BBC Science
http://www.bbc.co.uk/science/space/
British National Space Centre
http://www.bnsc.gov.uk/
European Space Agency
http://sci.esa.int/
**Star Child: A Learning Centre for
Young Astronomers**
http://starchild.gsfc.nasa.gov/

Books

Exploring the solar system: The Sun, Giles Sparrow
(Heinemann Library, 2001)
The Universe: The Sun, Raman Prinja
(Heinemann Library, 2002)

Useful address

London Planetarium
Marylebone Road
London
NW1 5LR

Index